Color Your Way Through Real Estate

A Kids Coloring Book

Danielle Andrews

Dedication

To my beloved son, Omri Andrews, you are the shining star whose creativity and imagination inspired every page of this book. Your curiosity about homes and love for coloring sparked the idea for this project, and I am forever grateful for your joyful spirit and endless inspiration.

To my dear husband, De'Garryan Andrews, your unwavering love, support, and encouragement made this book a reality. Thank you for being my rock and for believing in me every step of the way.

To all the children who will use this book and dream of becoming homeowners one day, may these pages ignite your imagination and inspire you to believe that all dreams are possible. This book is dedicated to each of you, with the hope that it brings joy, laughter, and a sense of wonder to your lives.

With love and gratitude,

Danielle Andrews

Directions

Welcome to the Andrews Family's Home buying Adventure!

In this coloring book, you are invited to join the Andrews family on their exciting journey to buying their first home. As you flip through the pages, you will discover different stages of the homebuying process, and your creativity will play a crucial role in making their dream home a reality.

Each page is filled with fun and interactive activities for you to enjoy. From coloring the exterior of the Andrews' future home, to decorating the interior rooms; your imagination is the key to bringing their new home to life.

Are you ready to help the Andrews family find their perfect home?

Grab your favorite colors and let your creativity soar as we make their homebuying journey unforgettable.

Stop 1: Let's Meet Our Realtor

A Realtor is a friendly special guide to help people find their home. They know lots of information about the neighborhoods in town. They are an important part of this adventure of finding a home.

Buying a home is a big job and I will need your help to guide the Andrews family in finding their new home. Join me on their journey.

Stop 2: The Bank

If you are going to buy a home, you will need money. Let's help the Andrews family get money from the bank to buy their new home.

Stop 3: House-Hunting

When it comes to buying a home, there are lots of options. Homes come in all types, sizes, and have many different things about them. Which home should the Andrews family choose. Pick your favorite home to color or color them all of you wish they could have all of the homes below.

Stop 3: House-Hunting (Continued)

There are other things people consider like how close the house is to parks, schools, malls, libraries, restaurants and more.

Stop 3: House-Hunting

Sometimes people find houses by going to open houses. This is when houses that are for sale are open and available for everyone to see. Many realtors host them to help the houses sell faster.

OPEN
HOUSE

Stop 4: You really like their house

When you're buying a house, you must let the seller know you want to buy their home by making an offer. This tells the seller we really like your house and want to make it your own. This is when you talk about how much you can pay and come to a fair agreement.

Stop 5: You want to make sure...

Houses should be safe and sound. We want to make sure it is a good place to sleep at night and make lots of great memories. Can you spot the safety features in this house? Color the fire extinguisher, security alarm, and smoke detectors different from the rest of the house.

Stop 6: You must protect it...

This is a big step! Houses are special just like you and when something is very special, we must protect it. A person called an appraiser comes to the house and looks at the house top to bottom to make sure it is as special as the Andrews family thinks it is.

Stop 7: Closing Day

Buying a house is important. So, there is a place that exists to sign all of the papers to make the house officially the Andrews family home. This place is called a title company.

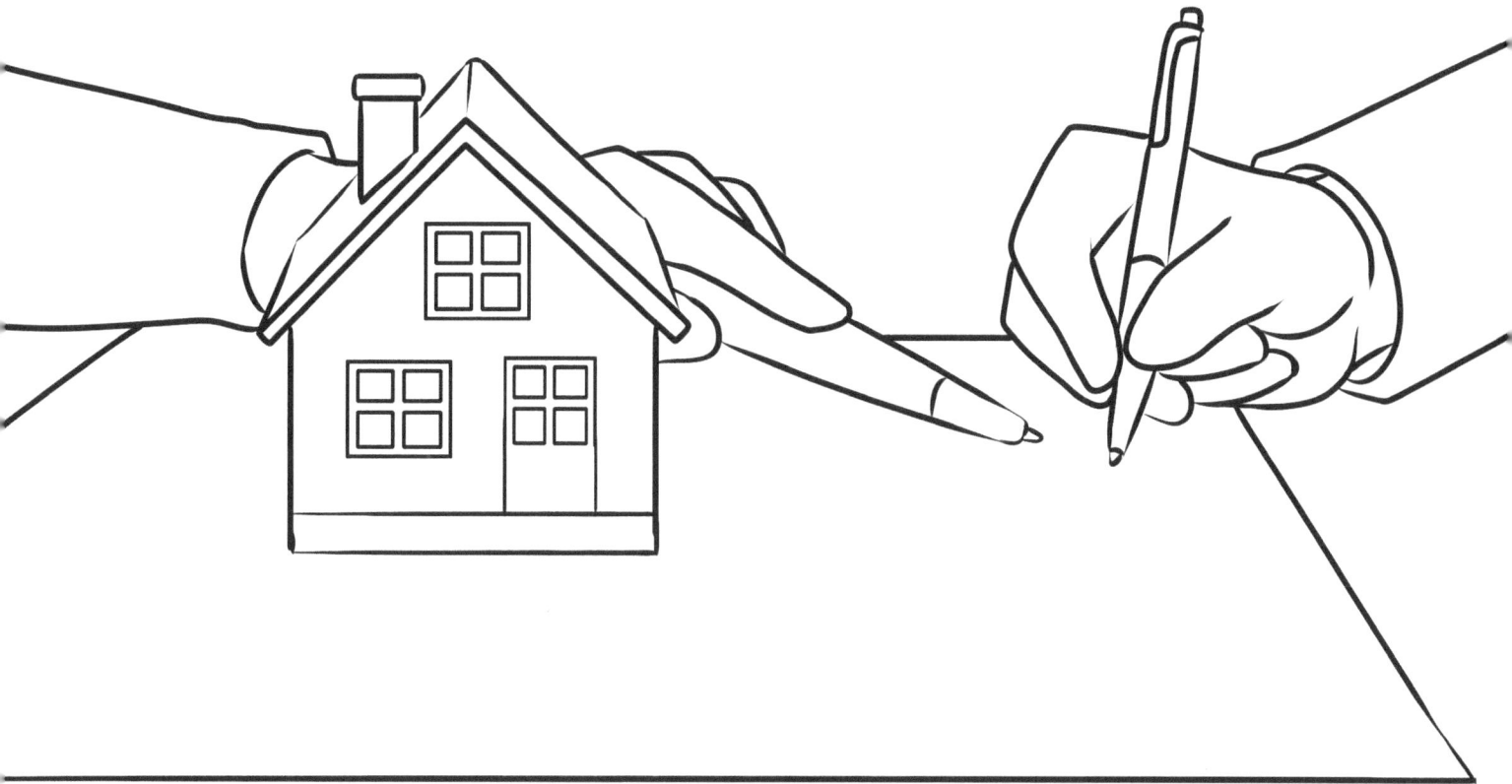

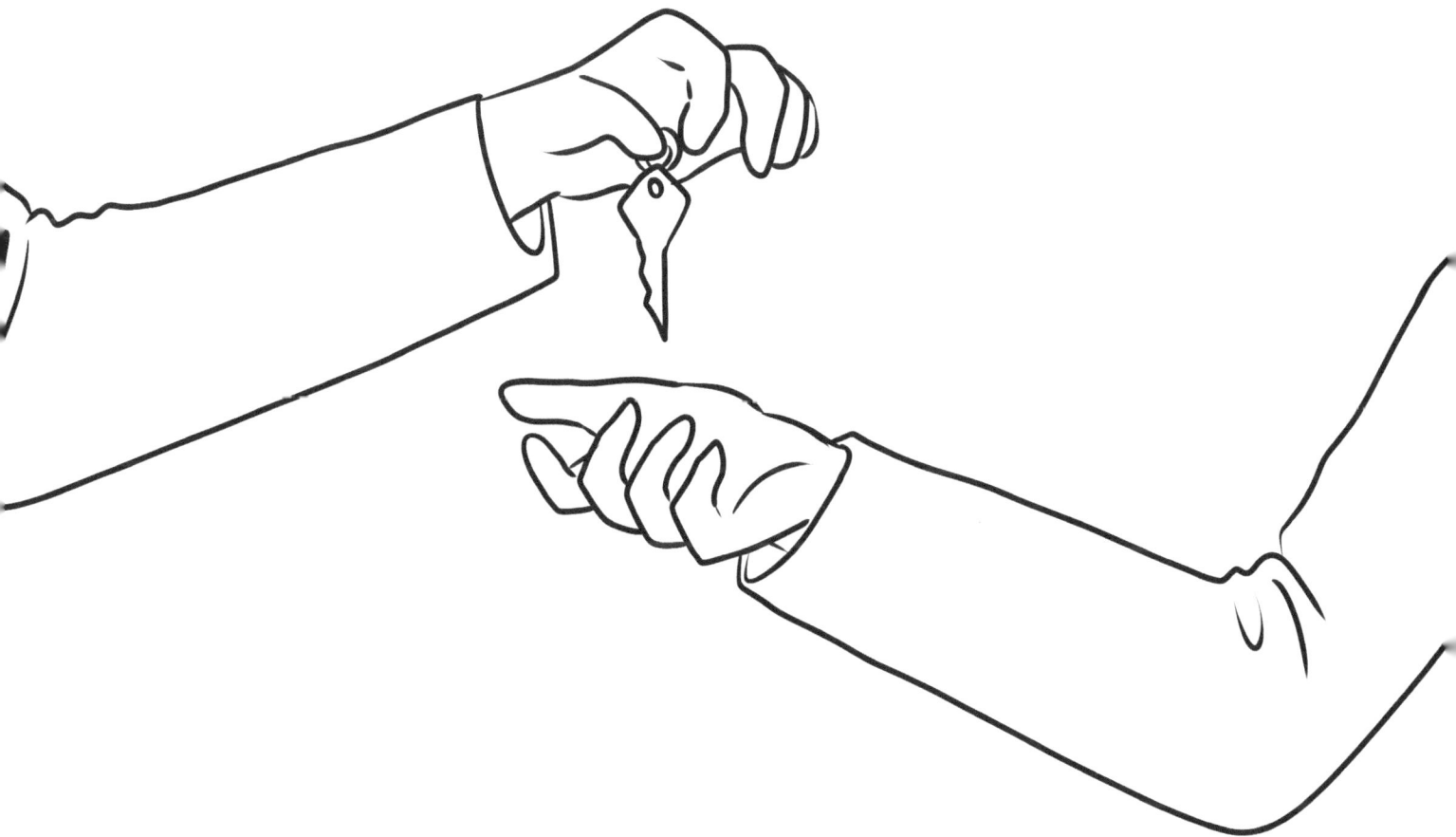

Step 8: Moving Day

Now that the Andrews family has the keys, it's time to move into their new home.

The Andrews family has found their new home and couldn't have done it without all of your help!

Now that they have found their new home, let's think about your future new home. Use the space below to draw what you imagine your home will look like one day.

Meet Danielle Andrews, a seasoned Real Estate Broker and passionate mom, whose love for both worlds inspired the creation of enchanting children's books. With a successful career in real estate, Danielle brings a unique perspective to the delightful tales within these pages.

As a devoted mother, she understands the importance of nurturing curiosity in young minds. Danielle is a wife to husband, De'Garryan Andrews, and mother to son, Omri Andrews, who is the catalyst for the creation of this book. Danielle is the Broker and Owner of Realty ONE Group Next Generation in Tallahassee, Florida. She is active in several community and professional organizations and loves to spread knowledge about the realties of the real estate industry.

Join Danielle on this imaginative journey, blending real estate expertise with the joy of parenthood, making learning a colorful adventure for your little ones.

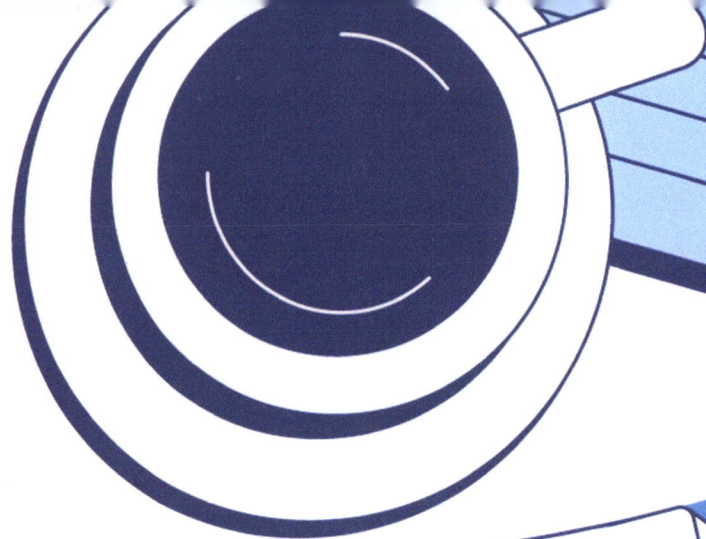

Glossary

Term	Definition
Appraisal	A report providing the amount a home is worth.
Appraiser	A licensed professional who performs a review of a home to determine how much it is worth.
Closing	This is when all the papers are signed and the new owner officially gets the keys to the house.
Mortgage	Money borrowed from a bank to purchase a home.
Open House	An event where people can come and look at a house that is for sale and decide if they would like to buy that house.
Realtor	A person who helps people buy and sell homes.
Title Company	A business that helps make sure the house you are buying is really yours. They also perform the closing when you are ready to finalize the purchase of your home.